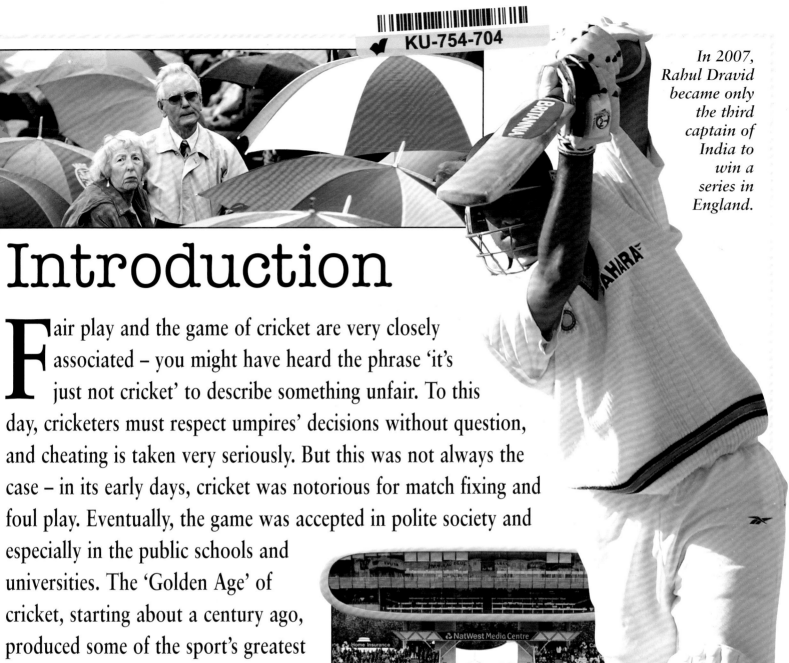

In 2007, Rahul Dravid became only the third captain of India to win a series in England.

Introduction

Fair play and the game of cricket are very closely associated – you might have heard the phrase 'it's just not cricket' to describe something unfair. To this day, cricketers must respect umpires' decisions without question, and cheating is taken very seriously. But this was not always the case – in its early days, cricket was notorious for match fixing and foul play. Eventually, the game was accepted in polite society and especially in the public schools and universities. The 'Golden Age' of cricket, starting about a century ago, produced some of the sport's greatest players. But by around 50 years ago, cricket, especially in Britain, was in decline. Then the rise of more superb players from the West Indies, and later, India and Pakistan, revived cricket all over the world, and it's still growing – as Ireland's success at the 2007 World Cup proved.

Broadcasters and journalists report on matches at Lord's from the vast Media Centre above the crowd.

History of the game

Would the earliest cricketers recognise the game being played these days in huge stadiums, and often under lights?

£1,000 was at stake in 1793 on the first Lord's Ground. The Earl of Winchelsea's XI competes against the Earl of Darnley's XI.

A PASTORAL PASTIME

Accounts of some form of cricket date back to the 1300s in England. 'Creckett' – one person aiming a ball at a target, perhaps a gate, a post or a stone, with another trying to hit the ball away with a stick – became a popular pastime in country districts. The first club was founded in the Hampshire village of Hambledon in about 1760. The best cricketers were village craftsmen and farmers, such as John and Richard Nyren at Hambledon. They developed batting and bowling styles that are still recognisable today.

HEADQUARTERS

Marylebone Cricket Club (MCC) was established at Lord's Ground in London at the end of the 18th century. Public schools, notably Eton, Harrow, Westminster and Winchester were playing in the 18th century, while the MCC drew up the first set of laws in 1835. Lord's remains the headquarters of cricket to this day.

The original Ashes urn (right) occupies pride of place in the MCC Cricket Museum at Lord's.

The game has always been popular in England's public schools where some of the best players in the game learned their craft. Eton have played Harrow regularly since 1818.

LORE AND LEGEND

Gambling and match fixing had been a major part of the game in its early days, but they were gradually stamped out by better regulation. William Clarke of Nottinghamshire formed the All-England XI in 1846, a collection of the best players who toured the country, playing matches and increasing cricket's popularity. The County Championship was formed in 1873 with nine counties playing each other on a regular basis – the start of First Class cricket. After several tours abroad, the first official Test match was played in Melbourne in 1877 between Australia and England.

ASHES TO ASHES

When Australia beat England in England for the first time in 1882, a mock obituary of English cricket was published, stating that 'the Body will be cremated and the Ashes taken to Australia'. When the Honourable Ivo Bligh captained England to victory in Australia the following winter, a group of ladies burnt a bail and placed the ashes in a tiny urn. The Ashes title is still fiercely played for today.

GOLDEN DAYS

W. G. Grace, who played top class cricket from 1865 to 1908, is still one of the most famous names of the game. A succession of fine cricketers followed in the first half of the 20th century. The best England side ever is said to have played in the 1902 series against Australia. Sir Jack Hobbs, who played for England between 1907 and 1930, and scored 197 first class centuries (100 runs or more), is one candidate for 'best batsman of all time'. But Sir Don Bradman, who averaged almost 100 runs every time he went into bat for Australia, is generally regarded as the best ever.

Two of Australia's finest ever batsmen – Sir Don Bradman (left) and Bill Ponsford are pictured on the 1934 tour of England.

THE MODERN GAME

Bradman's 1948 Australian team in England was known as the 'Invincibles'. More recently, powerful teams have emerged from the West Indies. Clive Lloyd's side of the 1970s and 1980s included fast bowlers Malcolm Marshall and Michael Holding and a great batsman in Viv Richards. The Australian team which won back 'The Ashes' in the 2006/07 series under Ricky Ponting is now regarded as one of the best of all time, with outstanding bowlers in Shane Warne and Glenn McGrath.

WACA ground at Perth, Western Australia, is considered to be one of the best in the world.

Kit

You may not have as much kit as a Test player, but you should use the best you can afford.

Bat-making in the early 20th century (right). The wood used for the blade is cricket bat willow, specially grown and matured. The main centres of the bat-making industry are Australia, England and India.

Winchester College team in the 1880s. Note the pads stuffed with horse hair, cane-handled bats and not a helmet in sight.

BATS ...

Today, there are several different designs of bat, but the most important aspect when choosing one is its balance. It must not be too heavy to prevent the playing of strokes, or too light. Professionals use a bat that weighs between 1.1 kg and 1.5 kg. Smaller batters usually prefer a short-handled bat, while taller players are usually more comfortable with a long handle.

Marcus Trescothick displays the contents of his 'coffin'.

KEY – 1 Kit case 2 Pads 3 Bats 4 England cap 5 Helmet 6 Thigh pad 7 Sun hat 8 Strips 9 Gloves 10 Fielding caps 11 Boots 12 Arm guard 13 Box

Balls have quartered outside casings of hide or leather, cortex centres and have always been hand-stitched. The seam and stitching help the ball swing in the air or move off the pitch.

TECH TIPS – KIT CARE
Look after your kit. If the grip on your bat wears out, have it replaced. Clean your pads and boots. Looking good at the wicket or in the field will not make you a county player, but it will boost your confidence.

BALLS ...

In First Class cricket, the ball should weigh no less than 155.9 g and no more than 163 g. In women's cricket, the minimum weight is 140 g, the maximum 151 g. Under-13 games are played with balls weighing between 133 g and 144 g.

Cricket probably requires more equipment than any other sport.

BAGGAGE ...

If your club has a communal kitbag, always try to pick out the same pads, gloves and bat, whether you're practising in the nets or for a match. You may not need six shirts and four pairs of trousers for each match like the pros, but the kit you do have, including gloves and a box (groin protector), should be comfortable.

... AND BOOTS

Without a good, well-made pair of boots, playing cricket could be a painful and uncomfortable experience. Years ago, top bowlers would invest in a pair of handmade boots. With the variety now on offer, few do that today, although fast bowlers often have part of a boot cut away to allow a big toe to peep through to prevent blistering.

1 Bowlers use boots with up to ten spikes, especially in damp conditions.
2 Half-spiked boots with rubber soles are worn on drier grounds.
3 Pimpled rubber soles may be more comfortable on hard grounds.

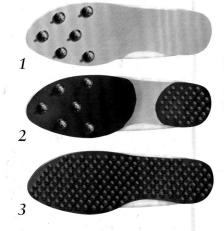

1

2

3

1850s BATSMAN does not wear pads or gloves, has crook-shaped bat and strip based on ordinary clothes (including top hat and neck tie).
1920s BATSMAN has a modern-shaped bat. Pads, abdominal protector and gloves are worn. A cap replaces the top hat.

2008

1850s

1920s

2008

1950s

2008 BATSMAN has more protection including helmet, arm guard, thigh pad and chest guard. Pads and gloves are thicker. He uses a heavier bat.
1950s KEEPER wears thick pads and gauntlet-type gloves.
2008 KEEPER wears large gloves with webbing, cut-down pads for free movement, a baseball-type cap and sunglasses.

Laws of the game

Every player should have a basic knowledge of the laws of the game, or you will never know when to appeal!

GAME AIMS

Batters aim to score more runs (points) than the opposition, by hitting the ball, then running between the wickets before the fielders can stop the ball (see page 13). Batters can be dismissed by being bowled out, when the ball hits part of the wicket; caught out, when the ball is caught directly off the bat without bouncing; stumped, when the wicketkeeper breaks the wicket, with the batter out of his ground (see page 22); run out, when the batter is attempting a run but fails to reach the wicket before it is broken; hit wicket, when the batter breaks his own wicket.

Scoreboards come in all shapes and sizes. In Australia, they give the names of all 22 players and the umpires, bowling figures, how the batters were out and for how many runs, when the wicket fell and, of course, the current score and number of overs.

THE UMPIRE'S JOB

The umpires are in charge of the game, deciding on whether the ground is fit for play, ruling on appeals by the fielding side, on fair and unfair play, counting the number of balls bowled and signalling to the scorers and players. One umpire stands behind the stumps at the bowler's end, the other may stand at point or square leg (see page 13), depending on where he can see best. Umpires consult each other when necessary.

Umpires Cowie and Venkat use a light meter to judge if play should stop due to bad light.

TECH TIPS – UMPIRE SIGNALS

Umpires use a code of signals to instruct players and scorers. A few of the more common signals are shown here.

HOWZAT?

Among the ways of dismissing a batter, leg before wicket (LBW) requires most explanation. The batter is out if the ball strikes him or her, not the bat, in the line between the wickets. If, in the umpire's opinion, the ball would have gone on to hit the stumps, the batter is given out on appeal by the fielding side, who shout 'howzat?' to the umpire.

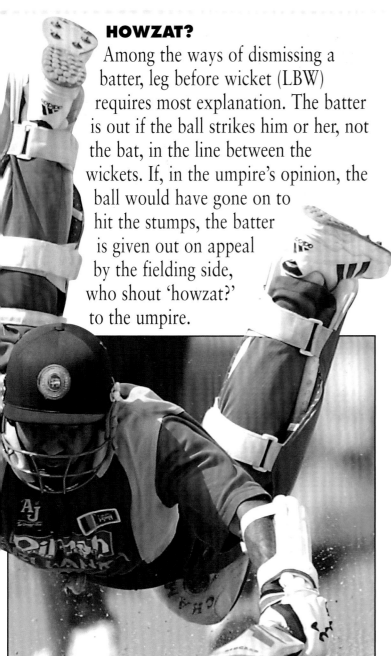

Run out? Howzat? The batter dives into his crease to try and make his ground, but the ball, thrown in by a fielder beats him to it. Call for the third umpire.

TECH TIPS – KEEPING SCORE

When cricket first started, the score was kept by cutting notches in a piece of wood. Scoring is more sophisticated now. A modern scorebook contains all the statistics of an innings, including the runs scored and details of the bowling.

A LITTLE HELP FROM MY FRIENDS

At Test level and in important First Class and one-day matches, more than two umpires are required. Modern technology means that decisions which are difficult for umpires to make in the middle can be quickly reviewed by a third umpire in the pavilion, studying a TV monitor. This way, a batter can be sure that when he is given out, he is definitely out.

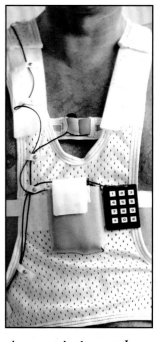

An umpire's vest has a microphone for communicating with the third umpire.

1 OUT – Batter loses wicket.
2 FOUR – Ball crosses boundary rope (see page 12).
3 SIX – Ball crosses rope without bouncing.
4 BYE – Run is scored without ball hitting bat.
5 LEG BYE – Ball misses bat, but hits batsman and run is scored.
6 NO-BALL – Bowler steps over popping crease or steps on return crease (see page 13).
7 WIDE – Bowled ball passes outside of return crease.

Pitch and positions

The first ten days of Lancashire's 2001 season at Old Trafford were completely washed out.

Cricket is played everywhere, from Test grounds like Lord's to the village green, but the fielding positions are the same.

THE PAVILION

Most First Class grounds in England have large pavilions, some built in Victorian days. They have two spacious dressing rooms for the teams, an umpires' room, a players' dining room, kitchen, members' bars and viewing areas. Club pavilions are much smaller.

PREPARING THE PITCH

It is the groundsman's job to prepare the pitch. This means much more than simply mowing the grass to keep it short. He must work on it through the closed season to keep it clear of weeds. When the weather allows, he rolls the square to keep it level and hard to provide an even bounce of the ball. He uses materials like marl to bind the soil to prevent the surface of the pitch from crumbling.

MATCH DAY

While professional players practise before a match begins, the ground staff are busy making sure the ground is ready for play. The pitch is mowed, then, at least half an hour before the start, the creases are marked out and the pitch is rolled for a maximum of seven minutes. The outfield is also mowed, the boundaries marked out, either with white paint, a rope or boards. Once all is ready for play, the umpires leave the pavilion for the middle.

THE BOUNDARY ROPE marks the line to determine fours or sixes. A six is scored if the batter hits the ball over the rope without bouncing. A four is scored if the ball bounces before the rope.

SIGHTSCREENS are painted white when a normal ball is in use, and covered in black when a white ball is used, to help the batters see the ball.

Lord's, with the pavilion on the left contrasting with the new grandstand 'up the slope'.

THE HEAVY ROLLER

The captain of the batting side decides before the start of each innings and before the start of each day, whether to have the pitch rolled. A heavy roller deadens a pitch, helping the opening batters against fast bowlers. But it could also make the pitch break up, benefiting the batting side's bowlers later on.

The Ahmedabad heavy roller – hard work for the ground staff.

THE SCOREBOARD *displays the score, number of wickets to have fallen and overs bowled. It may also show individual batter's scores. The official scorers are often positioned here.*

NETS *are for batting and bowling practice.*

THE COVERS *are brought on to the square to cover the pitch when it rains. Plastic sheets are used to cover the rest of the ground if necessary.*

THE PITCH *is 20.12 m long and at least 3.05 m wide. The wickets are set up at either end of the pitch.*

THE SQUARE *is the area where the pitches are prepared. Test grounds have room for 20 or more pitches, club grounds much fewer.*

Bails — 22.86 cm
Stumps
71.1 cm
1.22 m

THE WICKET

Bowling crease

Popping crease — 2.64 m

Return crease

TECH TIPS – FIELD PLACINGS

Positions are for a right-handed batter.

1 Wicketkeeper
2 First slip
3 Second slip
4 Third slip
5 Gully
6 Point
7 Silly point
8 Cover point
9 Extra cover
10 Mid-off
11 Mid-on
12 Long-off
13 Long-on
14 Silly mid-off
15 Silly mid-on
16 Short mid-wicket
17 Mid-wicket
18 Deep mid-wicket
19 Square leg
20 Deep square leg
21 Forward short leg
22 Short leg
23 Short square leg
24 Leg slip
25 Leg gully
26 Fine leg
27 Deep fine leg
28 Third man
29 Bowler
30 Batters
31 Umpire
32 Square leg umpire

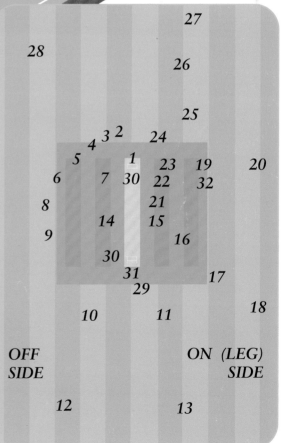

OFF SIDE

ON (LEG) SIDE

Batting – the basics

What is the key to becoming a good batter? The basic skill is to keep your eyes on the ball.

A STRAIGHT BAT

Playing the ball with a straight bat, perpendicular to the ground, gives you more chance of actually hitting the ball. Learn the basic defensive strokes first. You will probably use the forward defensive most often. For a right hander, from the balanced stance, plant your left foot forwards to where you think the ball will bounce. Moving your bat forwards at the same time alongside the pad ensures there is no way through for the ball to hit your stumps. Keep your head still and your eyes on the ball. For a backward defensive stroke, take the right foot back, keep your head and body in line with the ball, and again play with a straight bat. Most of the strokes you need in cricket are developed from the two basic defensive strokes.

Net practice – don't try to hit every ball to the other side of the ground. Play as you would in a match.

NETS

Even cricketers who play a reasonable standard of club cricket sometimes forget what net practice is for. It is to polish up your technique and get rid of faults. The most frequent fault is not watching the ball as it leaves the bowler's hand, through the air, pitching and on to the bat. It is not possible to focus on every ball received and play the correct shot – if it was, nobody would get out! But regular practice gives your brain a better chance of sending the right signals to your hands and feet.

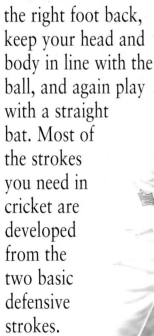

The forward defensive – left foot forward

TECH TIPS – STANCE AND GRIP

Lay the bat face downwards on the ground and pick it up as if you were picking up an axe. The way you are now holding the bat is the orthodox grip used by all the best players in the world, albeit sometimes with slight modifications. Whilst holding the bat, take up a stance with feet parallel to the popping crease and as wide apart as feels comfortable. Turn your head to face the bowler, so that you're looking over your shoulder.

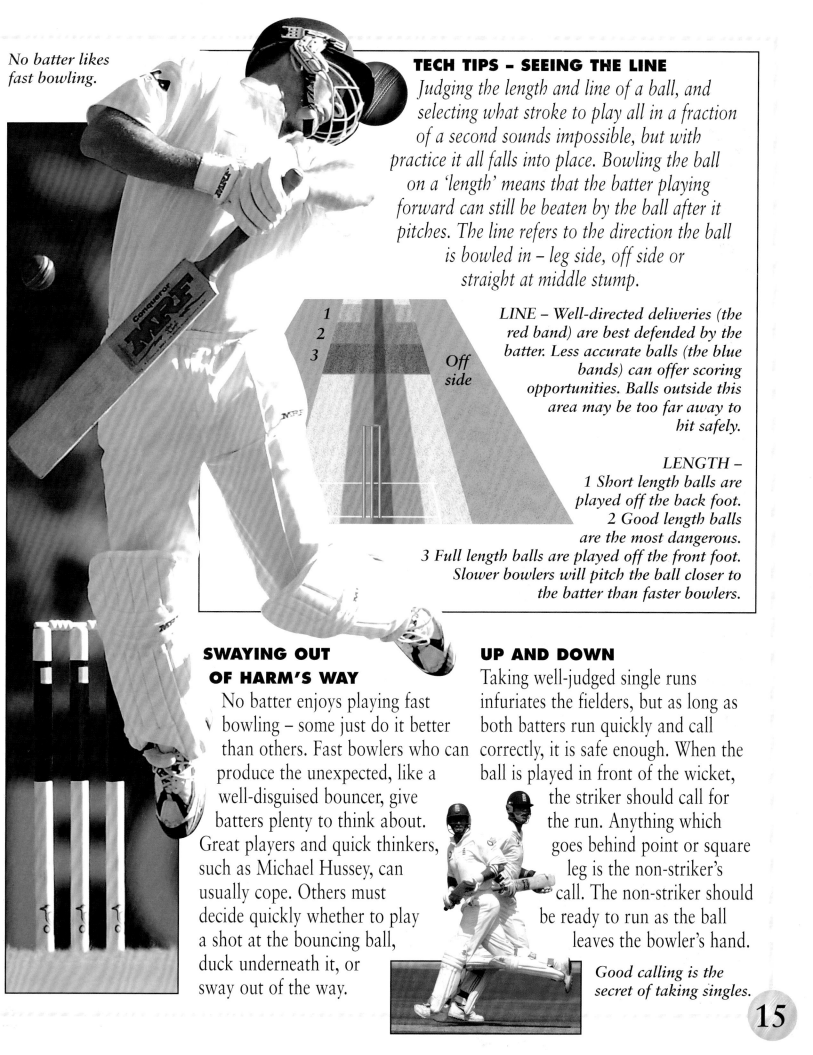

No batter likes fast bowling.

TECH TIPS – SEEING THE LINE

Judging the length and line of a ball, and selecting what stroke to play all in a fraction of a second sounds impossible, but with practice it all falls into place. Bowling the ball on a 'length' means that the batter playing forward can still be beaten by the ball after it pitches. The line refers to the direction the ball is bowled in – leg side, off side or straight at middle stump.

1
2
3

Off side

LINE – Well-directed deliveries (the red band) are best defended by the batter. Less accurate balls (the blue bands) can offer scoring opportunities. Balls outside this area may be too far away to hit safely.

LENGTH –
1 Short length balls are played off the back foot.
2 Good length balls are the most dangerous.
3 Full length balls are played off the front foot. Slower bowlers will pitch the ball closer to the batter than faster bowlers.

SWAYING OUT OF HARM'S WAY

No batter enjoys playing fast bowling – some just do it better than others. Fast bowlers who can produce the unexpected, like a well-disguised bouncer, give batters plenty to think about. Great players and quick thinkers, such as Michael Hussey, can usually cope. Others must decide quickly whether to play a shot at the bouncing ball, duck underneath it, or sway out of the way.

UP AND DOWN

Taking well-judged single runs infuriates the fielders, but as long as both batters run quickly and call correctly, it is safe enough. When the ball is played in front of the wicket, the striker should call for the run. Anything which goes behind point or square leg is the non-striker's call. The non-striker should be ready to run as the ball leaves the bowler's hand.

Good calling is the secret of taking singles.

15

Batting – scoring runs

Everybody wants to hit fours and sixes – that's why it's said that cricket is a batter's game.

TIMING

No matter what the sport, timing is all important, but nobody can teach you how to time a stroke. Practice is the only way to learn. Good timing means hitting the ball at the instant the bat comes through on the downswing at maximum speed. Some players never perfect the art of timing and instead rely on brute force, but they are rarely capable of playing a long innings.

FOOTWORK

For most strokes, one step forwards or backwards is enough to put the batter in position to play the shot. But when a bowler is making the ball spin, or tossing the ball higher in flight, more steps may be required to counter his action. So you may see a batter taking two or three steps down the pitch to try and hit the ball before it bounces – there is no way it can spin then!

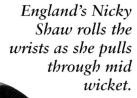

England's Nicky Shaw rolls the wrists as she pulls through mid wicket.

India's Rahul Dravid drives into the offside off the back foot.

TECH TIPS – SHOTS

Most players prefer batting mainly on the front foot or the back foot, but it is wise to be capable of playing enough strokes off either foot to beat the bowlers. The key to playing good cricket strokes is to watch the ball and keep the head still.

THE ON AND OFF DRIVE

With the front foot as close to the pitch of the ball as possible, swing the bat through the line of the ball, keeping your weight on the front foot, and follow through.

England's Charlotte Edwards expertly turning to leg.

SKILL DRILL – FINDING THE GAPS

For most average club players, finding the gaps in the field is just a matter of luck, but with practice, you can place your shots wide of the fielders.

1 Square cut
2 Off drive
3 On drive
4 Pull
5 Sweep

Leg side

Off side

OFF DRIVE DRILL
Place markers and fielders as shown. Aim to strike ball in shaded areas. Make sure deliveries are pitched up on the off side, and can be driven.

Orthodox front foot drive by Michael Vaughan

WORKING THE BALL AROUND

There will be times when the bowlers are so strong that you don't know where the next run is coming from. Encourage your batting partner to back up at the non-striker's end, and look for quick singles so you can draw the fielders in closer. Once they're in, you can hit the ball harder to penetrate the field.

TECH TIPS – LBW

If a ball passes the bat and hits the batter's body, he may be given out, 'leg before wicket'.

1 and 3 'out' – unless the batter's front foot is forward to the pitch of the ball or the ball hits a pad outside the line of off stump and a stroke is attempted.
2 and 4 'not-out' – the ball pitches in line with, but misses the stumps.
5 'not-out' – LBW laws do not apply to balls pitching outside the line of leg stump.

1
2
3
4
5

Leg side

Line of stumps

THE SQUARE CUT
When you spot a delivery that is short and wide of the off stump, rock on to the back foot. Hit the ball with arms at full stretch.

THE PULL
Move towards the off side to be inside the line of flight. Keep the ball down, by rolling the wrist as the shot is played.

THE SWEEP
Front foot down the pitch, back knee to the ground, the bat comes down and across to the ball. A roll of the wrist keeps it down and directs the shot backwards.

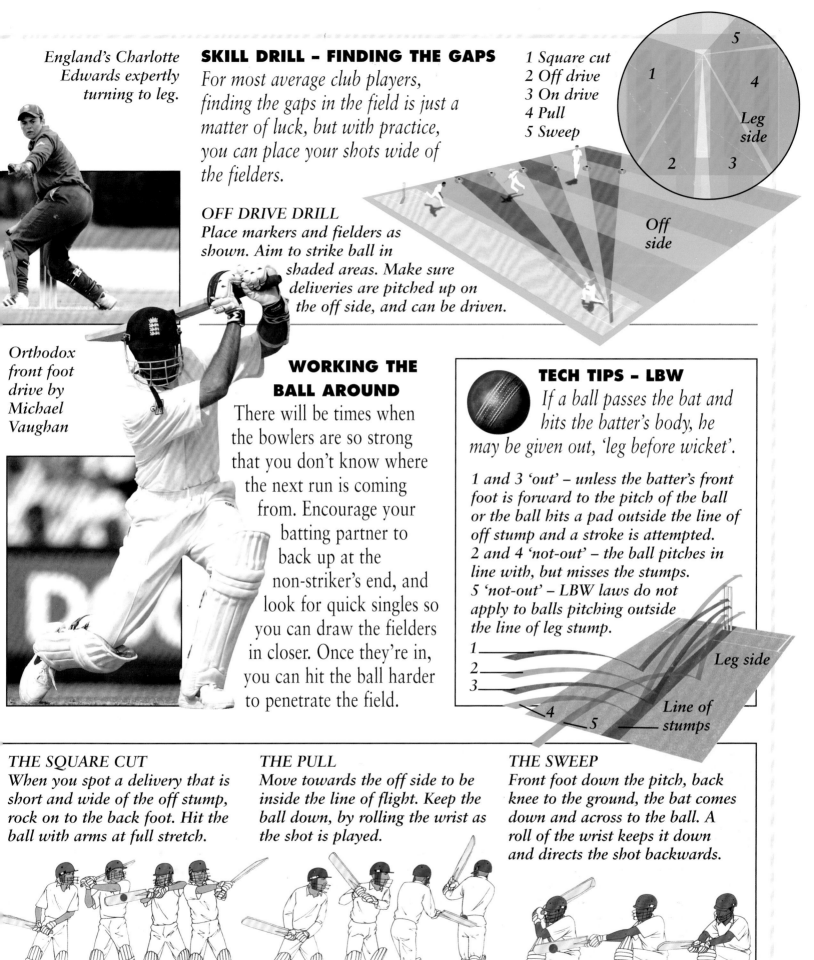

Bowling – seam

As a bowler, you have a chance to beat the opposition with every ball.

THE RUN UP

Fast bowling requires fitness and control. Your run up should let you arrive at the bowling crease balanced and at sufficient speed. Bowl side on, as close to the stumps as possible. Look over your front shoulder with your leading arm stretched upwards, focusing on the point you want the ball to bounce. Release the ball with your arm as high as possible. Complete the action with a full 180-degree turn of the shoulders. If you feel strained, slow down.

Brett Lee of Australia looks balanced before powering down another 145 km/h delivery.

Even at full speed, England's Matthew Hoggard concentrates on where he wants to pitch the ball.

TECH TIPS – BALL CONTROL

Even if you have the ability to bowl fast, it is useless unless you can pitch the ball in the right place. Once you can do that, try a few variations to your standard delivery to keep the batter thinking.

1 2 3 4 5

1 *Feet, hips and shoulders point same way.*
2 *Turn body side on to target.*
3 *Arms start 'windmill' action.*
4 *Pivot off front foot to create pace.*
5 *After ball is released, move off wicket.*

BASIC GRIP Wrist forwards – angling the seam can make the ball move off the pitch.

OFF CUTTER As the ball is released, the fingers move down the side to generate spin.

LEG CUTTER Fingers work down the other side of ball from the off cutter.

THE DELIVERY

Seam bowlers try to bang the ball hard into the pitch, landing it on its seam so that it moves late off the surface to beat the batter. Leg cutters and off cutters take time to perfect. For most young seam bowlers, the best strategy is to grip the ball with the seam upright, then aim to hit the pitch with the ball bouncing on the seam. That's as good a way to confuse batters as any other.

India's Ishant Sharma after bowling remains focused on the ball – there may be a return catch!

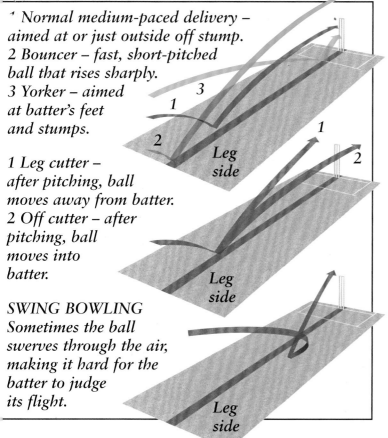

1 Normal medium-paced delivery – aimed at or just outside off stump.
2 Bouncer – fast, short-pitched ball that rises sharply.
3 Yorker – aimed at batter's feet and stumps.

1 Leg cutter – after pitching, ball moves away from batter.
2 Off cutter – after pitching, ball moves into batter.

SWING BOWLING
Sometimes the ball swerves through the air, making it hard for the batter to judge its flight.

TECH TIPS – NO-BALLS AND WIDES

It is no use bowling to prevent the scoring of runs, only then to send down a flurry of wides and no-balls, destroying all the previous good work. Control, both of the direction of the ball and of the bowling action, is essential.

A no-ball is called if all of the bowler's front foot is over the popping crease, or part of the back foot is touching the return crease when the ball is bowled.

THE FOLLOW THROUGH

If you have achieved the full 180-degree rotation of the shoulders in the delivery stride, the follow through should take care of itself. After bowling, don't pull up suddenly, but allow your momentum to take you off the pitch, gradually slowing down over four or five metres. Eyes on the ball, be ready to change direction if the batter hits back a return catch.

Ryan Sidebottom of Notts and England follows through in his delivery stride.

19

Bowling – spin

Spin bowling is more than just slow bowling – spinners cleverly vary and disguise their deliveries. There are two main types of spin bowling.

India's Harbhajan Singh - 'The Turbanator' – delights his team with the dismissal of the Australian captain.

WRIST SPIN (LEG SPIN)

Wrist spinners have always enjoyed success on the hard, dusty pitches of the Indian subcontinent and Australia. Because of the nature of their action, it used to be thought that they bowled too many bad balls, especially early in a spell. Shane Warne proved that did not have to be the case, with his disguised variations of the standard leg break.

FINGER SPIN (OFF SPIN)

Off spinners are common in England where pitches are slow and lack bounce. In club cricket they are often damp too, so as they dry out, an off spinner gains some grip and turn. Spinners may look casual, but to make the ball spin, they have to rip their fingers across the seam. For a right-handed bowler, this action starts with the left shoulder facing down the wicket and rotating to bring the right shoulder through.

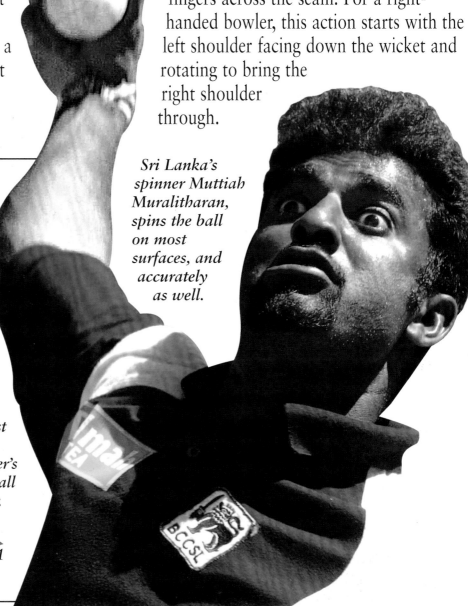

Sri Lanka's spinner Muttiah Muralitharan, spins the ball on most surfaces, and accurately as well.

TECH TIPS – THE TURNING BALL

As a basic rule, wrist spinners are trying to turn the ball away from the bat. Off spinners attempt the opposite.

1 The leg break is the leg spinner's normal delivery, with the ball turning away from the batter.
2 A 'googly' turns into the batter, but uses leg break 'action'.
3 A 'flipper' does not turn, but it's fast and keeps low.
4 The off break is the off spinner's normal delivery, with the ball turning into the batter.

1
2
3
4

Line of stumps

Leg side

TECH TIPS – GOING FOR A SPIN

Try to master the basic deliveries of leg and off spin. Wrist spinners in particular need to practise a great deal to land the ball in the right spot on the pitch consistently.

WRIST SPIN

1 As arm swings over, wrist turns outwards ...
2 ... showing back of hand to batter.
3 Palm faces upwards as ball is released, spin generated through turning wrist and grip.

FINGER SPIN

1 Ball held with first and second fingers across seam.
2 At moment of release, first and second fingers work down seam, giving ball spin.

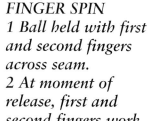

1   **2**   **3**   **1**   **2**

TACTICS

Slow bowlers have to be crafty to get wickets, but there are some tactics which can be used, legally, to help them on their way. Bowling the occasional ball from behind the bowling crease rather than up on the popping crease often confuses a batter.

Monty Panesar England's wily left arm spinner.

THE ART OF DISGUISE

A spinner who simply bowls one basic delivery is soon found out by a quick-thinking batter. Try to vary deliveries, use slower and quicker balls, but with the same action. Leg spinners should develop the googly, the off spinner bowled with a leg break action – difficult, but not impossible. Saqlain Mushtaq of Pakistan, an off spinner, regularly dismisses batsmen with a leg break that seems to be an off break.

Michael Clarke of Australia – a fine batsman but also a more than useful left arm spinner who has often taken valuable wickets for his team.

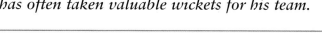

SKILL DRILL – HITTING THE SPOT

You may hear that a slow bowler has been 'hit off his length' by a particular batter. This could be because, instead of concentrating on where he is pitching the ball, he is watching the batter's movements. Practise pitching on a length like this.

Place a metal tray on the length you wish to bowl. You'll soon hear it when you've found your range.

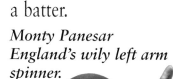

Leg side

Line of stumps

21

Wicketkeeping

T he wicketkeeper can make an average fielding side look good, or he or she can make a good fielding side ineffective.

Howzat? The wicketkeeper is in the best position to judge when to appeal for LBW.

STANDING UP AND STANDING BACK

Wicketkeepers probably cover more ground in an innings than any other fielder. When standing back to a quick bowler, the keeper should always be running up to the stumps, to take returns from fielders. When standing up to the stumps for a slow bowler, he or she may have to dart round in front of the batter, to field and prevent the short single. Most good, close catchers could do an adequate job standing back. But the quality of the keeper is best judged standing up close to the spinners.

Stumped! The batsman is out of his ground – beyond the popping crease.

TECH TIPS – STUMPING

Wicketkeepers and slow bowlers have always worked in partnership – like Gilchrist and Warne, or Dhoni and Harbhajan today. A wicketkeeper must always know what the spinner is trying to do, and that takes practice together.

It's a crime to waste the chance of a stumping. The keeper can't take the ball until it has passed the stumps, unless it has hit the bat or the batter. If the batter's back foot is outside the popping crease, whip the bails off quickly and smoothly.

For both stumping and run-outs, the ball has to be in the hand that breaks the wicket to count, unlike here.

THE KEEPER AND THE SLIP CORDON

As the slip fielders take up their positions in relation to the wicketkeeper, he or she must never stand too far back. If the keeper is taking deliveries from fast bowlers down by his or her toes, the ball is unlikely to carry to a slip standing even further back.

Good wicketkeepers watch the ball all the way from the bowler's hand, off the pitch and into the gloves.

India's star Mahendra Dhoni – a fine wicketkeeper and dashing batsman.

AGILITY

Wicketkeepers come in all shapes and sizes, but they must have stamina and agility to keep on the move throughout an innings. A keeper who only takes balls that come straight through is no help to the team.

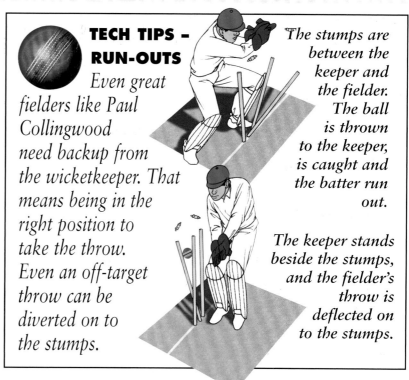

TECH TIPS – RUN-OUTS

Even great fielders like Paul Collingwood need backup from the wicketkeeper. That means being in the right position to take the throw. Even an off-target throw can be diverted on to the stumps.

The stumps are between the keeper and the fielder. The ball is thrown to the keeper, is caught and the batter run out.

The keeper stands beside the stumps, and the fielder's throw is deflected on to the stumps.

ANTICIPATION

Close fielders never anticipate, but wicketkeepers must. The quicker the keeper can judge where the ball is going after it has pitched, the easier the job is. Like a slip fielder, stay semi-crouched for as long as possible, trying to keep your eyes on the same level as the bounce of the ball. Go for everything within reason. So many brilliant catches have been taken by keepers when nobody thought they had a chance.

Fielding

As the old saying goes, 'catches win matches'. That's perfectly true, though fielding balls on the ground is just as important in keeping the pressure on the batting side.

Try for everything – a good stop saves runs and could make all the difference.

SETTING A FIELD

Of all the ways in which a batter can be dismissed, 'caught' is by far the most frequent. Think about where to place fielders. It is not much use having three slips and a gully if you don't have a fast bowler who can move the ball away from the bat. If you have a fielder who can run like a greyhound and throw accurately, don't put him at fine leg. Fielders of that type should be in the covers, or lurking 'around the corner' on the leg side to make the batters think twice about going for a run.

THE SPECIALISTS

These days, virtually every position is a specialist position. But years ago, good catchers fielded in the slips and the rest scattered. Players like Derek Randall in the 1970s changed all that, when he perfected the art of cover fielding, running in as the bowler approached, so that he was on the move the moment the ball was hit. A chase to the boundary usually meant a slide across the turf to pull the ball back.

Like tigers in the slips, Australia's cordon stands poised, waiting for the edge which will eventually come off their fast bowlers.

TECH TIPS – CATCHING

Not everybody can field in the slips, and a catch in the outfield could prove just as vital. Try the 'baseball method' of catching away from the bat. Fingers up, but not so the view is obscured, take the ball into the chest. Closer to the wicket, the catch might just be lobbed up. Fingers down, extend the arms and get underneath the catch, but again take it into the body and hold on.

Fingers up

Fingers down

South Africa's Andre Nel – eyes on the ball – dives forward to take a catch.

GROUNDWORK

It's vital to keep the runs scored at a minimum. If you're in the outfield, anticipate where the batter will hit the ball and start to move in that direction. Keep your eyes on the ball, right from the bowler's hand on to the bat. Throw in with your weight on the back foot and follow through.

Throwing from the boundary – point the left arm at the target.

CATCHES WIN MATCHES

Slip fielders have an exciting job, hanging on to fast travelling snicks. First slip crouches and watches the ball from the bowler's hand on to the edge of the bat and relies on co-ordination between eyes and hands. Second slip, and those wider towards gully, usually concentrate on the edge of the bat.

SKILL DRILL – RUN-OUTS

Fielders must always be looking for run-outs. This drill will help sharpen reflexes and throwing accuracy. Four or more fielders stand in a 30 m circle, with the stumps at the centre. A feeder is placed next to the stumps.

3 Other fielders are ready to back up missed attempts.

15 m

2 Fielder picks up and throws the ball at stumps in one movement.

1 Feeder hits the ball to one side of any fielder.

TECH TIPS – FIELDING THE BALL

There is nothing worse than fielding a simple rolling ball on the boundary and missing it, costing your side runs. Whenever possible, use the 'long barrier'.

Go down on one knee. Watch the ball carefully, stay side-on to it and keep the hands together – your legs should act as a barrier if the ball suddenly bounces up.

25

Cricket variations

There is more to the game than Test cricket – it doesn't have to last five days and be played in vast stadiums.

Kwik Cricket – not a Test match, but it's just as infuriating when you get out!

THE PYJAMA GAME

Until the 1970s, cricket was a game played in all-white kit, with red leather balls and white sightscreens. That largely remains the case, but professional sides now often play one-day matches in coloured kit. The World Cup is now a 'pyjama game', as are one-day, limited-over internationals and domestic competitions. Although England was responsible for introducing the professional one-day game in 1962, the side has rarely threatened to dominate the international version.

Sri Lankan batsman Kumar Sangakkara watches as Nathan Bracken bowls for Australia in the 2007 Cricket World Cup final.

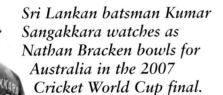

KWIK CRICKET

This game was introduced about 20 years ago, to give younger children an idea of how cricket is played. Played with a soft ball and shortened pitch, it does not require any expensive equipment, such as pads and boots, and can be played by anyone of any age. It gives youngsters a chance to experience batting, bowling and fielding.

The Wanderers' Stadium in Johannesburg was a dramatic setting for the opening match of the first World Twenty20 Cup in 2007 when the hosts met the West Indies.

DAY/NIGHT MATCHES

Australia introduced the first day/night games on a regular basis, when it was thought that interest in the regular version was flagging. It soon caught on, and the major grounds were equipped with permanent floodlights. An even shorter and more dynamic version of the game was introduced in England in 2003 – Twenty20. Nowadays international matches are played all over the world. With just 20 overs a side, batters have no time to 'play themselves in' - it's action from the very first delivery.

TECH TIPS – ONE-DAY FIELDING RESTRICTIONS

Fielding restrictions in the first 15 overs of 50-over innings mean that only two fielders are allowed to be outside the outer markers. Of those inside the ring, at least two, other than the wicketkeeper, must be in catching positions inside the inner circles.

All but two of the fielding side are within the 'ring' for the first 15 overs.

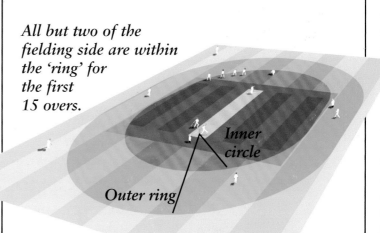

Inner circle

Outer ring

The world of cricket

Cricket is growing in popularity and the successful, inaugural Twenty20 World Cup in South Africa brought the game to a new, younger audience.

Sachin Tendulkar started on the beach in the Indian subcontinent.

UNIVERSAL APPEAL

The International Cricket Council governs the world game on behalf of over 100 member countries. The ten test-playing nations have been joined by the likes of Afghanistan, Slovenia and Thailand recently.

THE WORLD CUP

Though hardly as popular as the football and rugby equivalents, the cricket World Cup has become an important competition since its introduction in 1975. Held every four years, the winners have been Australia (1987, 1999, 2003 and 2007), India (1983), Pakistan (1991), Sri Lanka (1995) and the West Indies (1975 and 1979). England have never won the trophy, although they have been in the final on three occasions. The game between India and Pakistan in the 2003 World Cup was televised in over 180 countries – the most watched cricket match of all time.

Australia's captain Ricky Ponting lifts the ICC World Cup after the 2007 final against Sri Lanka in Barbados.

TROPHIES AND TOURNAMENTS

The England-Australia series for the Ashes is the oldest competition in Test cricket, while the County Championship in England started officially in 1890. Australia's First Class competition, now known as the Pura Cup, began as the Sheffield Shield in 1892. In late 2007 the setting up of the unofficial Indian Cricket League as a rival to the proposed Indian Premier League's Twenty20 competition caused controversy in the game, but also showed the amount of interest, backed by wealthy investors, that there is in present day cricket.

The modern Ashes trophy is slightly larger and flashier than the original (see page 6).

WOMEN'S CRICKET

The first women's test match was staged in Brisbane in 1934 when Australia played England. With New Zealand, just three countries played women's test cricket until 1976 when India met New Zealand, regularly playing in front of crowds of up to 40,000. The first Women's World Cup was held in 1973 (two years before the men's) and was won by England who also lifted the trophy in 1993. But overall the women's game, now played in over 70 countries, has been dominated by Australia.

Australia has won the Women's World Cup five times.

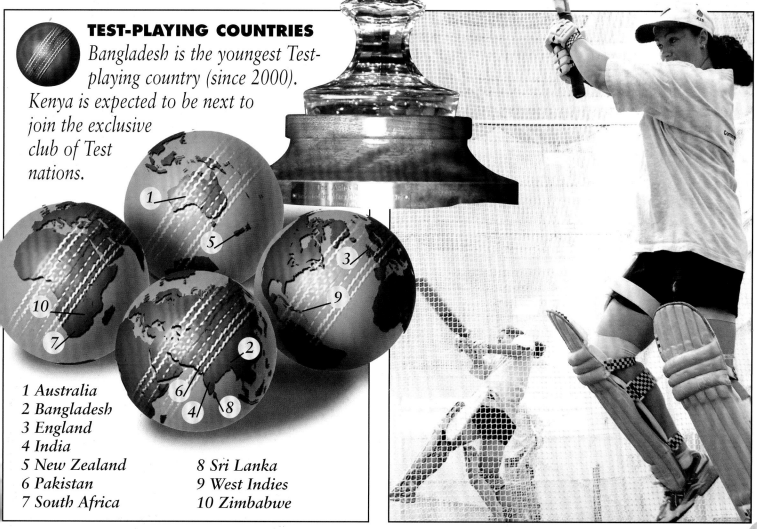

TEST-PLAYING COUNTRIES

Bangladesh is the youngest Test-playing country (since 2000). Kenya is expected to be next to join the exclusive club of Test nations.

1 *Australia*
2 *Bangladesh*
3 *England*
4 *India*
5 *New Zealand*
6 *Pakistan*
7 *South Africa*
8 *Sri Lanka*
9 *West Indies*
10 *Zimbabwe*

29

Staying fit

As cricket is a stop-start game, it is easy to pull a muscle through not being properly warmed up.

HEALTHY EATING

Try to keep to a balanced diet by eating foods from the basic groups – dairy products, meat, fish and chicken, fruit and vegetables, plus cereals to absorb enough vitamins and calories. On match days, eat about two hours before the start. At lunch or tea, eat salads or fruit, nothing stodgy and drink plenty of liquids. In the professional game, drinks intervals are scheduled every hour.

EXERCISE

Good general fitness can only benefit your game. Bowlers, especially fast bowlers, should strengthen their legs by lapping the outfield. Estimate how far you would run during a normal bowling spell and lap the ground for an equivalent distance. Batters can also increase their stamina by running, swimming, cycling and gym work.

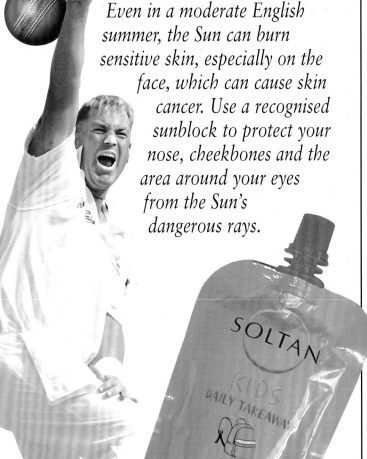

TECH TIPS – WAR PAINT

Even in a moderate English summer, the Sun can burn sensitive skin, especially on the face, which can cause skin cancer. Use a recognised sunblock to protect your nose, cheekbones and the area around your eyes from the Sun's dangerous rays.

Shane Warne is protected against the Sun, and a fearsome sight for a timid batsman.

Hip and leg stretch – holding the foot gently, pull backwards to stretch the upper thigh. Hold the leg with both hands below the knee and gently pull up towards the head to stretch the back of the thigh and loosen the hips.

Shoulder stretch – hook the right arm under the left elbow and gently pull back towards the head, stretching your left shoulder. Repeat with the other arm.

SKILL DRILL – STRETCHING

Warming up and warming down exercises are widely used by all the top teams, and not just before and after the match. During the game you can make sure you are ready to play an innings by using the stretching exercises on the left. In the field, even simple exercises, such as pushing the hands together for six seconds, work one muscle group against another. In this case, you can warm the muscles in your chest, arms and shoulders. Relax for 20 seconds and then repeat.

Glossary

APPEAL shout used to appeal to the umpire for LBW, stumped or run out – usually 'howzat?'

BAIL one of two cross-pieces on top of stumps

BOUNCER short bowling delivery which rears up at the batter

CORTEX hard, solid centre of the ball, around which the outer casing is stitched

CREASE lines at either end of the pitch

HOWZAT? 'how is that' – shout made in appeal

INNINGS either one batter's stay at the wicket, or the whole batting side's term at the wicket

MARL clay soil used on a pitch to ensure the surface binds together

NETS practice area surrounded by netting, where bowlers and batters can develop their skills in a confined area

OVER six successive deliveries bowled by the same bowler

RUN score credited to the batting team, if the striker and non-striker run to the opposite ends of the pitch without being run out or caught

RUN-OUT when a batter's wicket is broken as he or she is attempting a run

SNICK a delivery edged by the bat

STUMP three stumps and two bails make up the wicket. Or, the wicketkeeper can 'stump' a batter by breaking the wicket, with the batter out of his or her crease.

TEST MATCH five-day game played between two of the top ten countries

WICKET three stumps and bails at either end of the pitch, or another word for 'pitch'. A batter who has 'lost his wicket' is out.

Further information

England and Wales Cricket Board (ECB)
Lord's Ground,
London,
NW8 8QZ
www.ecb.co.uk
www.ecb.co.uk/womens/

Marylebone Cricket Club
Lord's Ground,
London,
NW8 8QN
www.lords.org

English Schools' Cricket Association
38 Mill House,
Woods Lane,
Hull,
HU16 4HQ

Australian Cricket Board
90 Jolimont Street,
Jolimont,
VIC 3002
Tel: (+613) 9653 9999
www.acb.com.au

Australian Institute of Sport
Leverrier Crescent,
Bruce,
ACT 2617
Tel: (+612) 6214 1369
www.ausport.gov.au/

Cricket Scotland
National Cricket Academy
Ravelston,
Edinburgh,
EH4 3NT
www.cricketeurope4.net/
SCOTLAND/home.shtml

Index

Afghanistan 28
All-England XI 6
Ashes 6, 7, 29
Australia 6, 7, 10, 15, 18, 20, 24

Bangladesh 29
Barbados 28
batting 14–17
Bligh, the Honourable Ivo 6
bowling 18–21
Bradman, Sir Don 7
Brisbane 29

Clarke, Michael 21
Clarke, William 6
Collingwood, Paul 23
County Championship 6, 29

Dhoni, Mahendra 22, 23
dismissal 10, 11
Dravid, Rahul 5, 16

Earl of Darnley's XI 6
Earl of Winchelsea's XI 6
Edwards, Charlotte 17
England 6, 7, 26, 28, 29
Eton College 6

fair play 5
fielding 24–25, 27
First Class cricket 6, 9, 12

Gilchrist, Adam 22
Grace, W. G. 7

Harrow School 6
Hobbs, Sir Jack 7
Hoggard, Matthew 18

Holding, Michael 7

India 5, 16, 20, 28, 29
Indian Cricket League 29
International Cricket Council
   (ICC) 28
'Invincibles', the 7
Ireland 5

Johannesburg 27

Kenya 29
kit 8–9
kwik cricket 26

laws 10–11
Lee, Brett 18
leg before wicket (LBW) 11, 17
Lloyd, Clive 7
Lord's Ground 5, 6, 12

Marshall, Malcolm 7
Marylebone Cricket Club
   (MCC) 6
McGrath, Glenn 7
Muralitharan, Muttiah 20
Mushtaq, Saqlain 21

Nel, Andre 25
New Zealand 29
Nottinghamshire 6
Nyren, John and Richard 6

one-day cricket 26

Pakistan 5, 19, 21, 28, 29
Panesar, Monty 21
pitch 12–13
Ponsford, Bill 7

Ponting, Ricky 7, 28
positions 12–13
Pura Cup 29

Randall, Derek 24
Richards, Viv 7

scoring 11
Sharma, Ishant 19
Shaw, Nicky 16
Sheffield Shield 29
Sidebottom, Ryan 19
Singh, Harbhajan 20, 22
Slovenia 28
South Africa 25, 28, 29
Sri Lanka 20, 26, 28, 29
Switzerland 28

Test cricket 6, 10, 11, 12, 26, 27, 28, 29
Thailand 28
Trescothick, Marcus 8
Twenty20 27, 28

umpire 10, 11

Vaughan, Michael 17

Warne, Shane 7, 20, 22, 30
West Indies 5, 7, 28, 29
Westminster School 6
wicketkeeping 22–23
Winchester College 6, 8
women's cricket 9, 17, 29
Women's World Cup 29
World Cup 26, 28

Zimbabwe 29